yes, we can! He Can HEAL

ARTS & LITERACY

QUARRY

yes, we can! He Can HEAL

ARTS & LITERACY

Inspiring Stories of Men Who Changed the World

JONATHAN JURAVICH
2023 National Elementary Art Teacher of the Year
RICHARD V. REEVES
Founder of the American Institute for Boys and Men

QUARRY

Quarto.com

This library edition published in 2026 by Quarry Books,
an imprint of The Quarto Group.
100 Cummings Center, Suite 265-D, Beverly, MA 01915, USA.
T (978) 282-9590 F (978) 283-2742

Distributed in the United States and Canada by Lerner Publisher Services
241 First Avenue North
Minneapolis, MN 55401 U.S.A.
www.lernerbooks.com

First Library Edition

Library of Congress Cataloging-in-Publication Control Number: 2025031595

Printed in China

10 9 8 7 6 5 4 3 2 1

For Ari and Josie, who remind me
to seek joy in life's small moments.
—JJ

For Bryce, an inspiring educator
and cherished son.
— RR

Contents

Arts

Literacy

Introduction

My youngest son, Cameron, was about six. I was driving him home after seeing the doctor. We were quiet for a time. Then he said, "Dad, I didn't know men could be doctors."

The doctor we had just seen was a man. But I realized that until that day, every doctor he had ever seen had been a woman. So it was not silly for him to think that being a doctor was something only women did.

But stop to consider this for a moment. That's amazing progress. Women were not even allowed to be doctors for most of human history! For women to be the only doctors in Cameron's world shows how relatively quickly and overwhelmingly stereotypes can be overcome.

I told Cameron then, and I am telling you now, yes, men can be doctors! But just as important, men can be *nurses*, too. Maybe that one sounds strange to you because most nurses are still women. But there are thousands of amazing nurses who are men. It is a great job for a man, and do not let anybody tell you otherwise! There are no rules about what jobs men can do.

This book series is about the sorts of jobs that are sometimes wrongly seen as jobs for women but are just as much for men.

Back during that car ride with Cameron, we talked about teachers. There were no men teaching at his elementary school, so he was not sure men could do that job either. In most countries, fewer men are teaching today than they used to. In the United States, only 23 percent of teachers are men now, compared with 33 percent in 1980.

But men can be teachers! In fact, I think we need men teaching and coaching in our schools more than ever.

Maybe you are more interested in STEM jobs, in which case, great! But maybe not. Maybe you are more interested in working with people, which is great, too. These are what I call "HEAL" subjects and jobs: in health, education, arts, and literacy. Nurses, teachers, childcare workers, therapists, social workers, assistants, psychologists: These are all HEAL jobs.

In recent years, girls have been encouraged to believe that they can be anything they want. That includes jobs that people once thought were "men's jobs." Now there are almost as many women as men working as doctors, lawyers, and scientists. Women fly fighter planes, fight fires, and pass laws. Maybe you even know some of them. This is amazing and wonderful.

But adults have not done as well yet showing that men can also do the things that are still thought of as "women's jobs," mostly in those HEAL professions. Just like girls used to be told that math or science was not right for girls, today boys too often get the message that nursing or social work or teaching are not "manly," or something equally stupid.

So, I am going to be honest with you. Right now it takes some courage to say you are thinking about one of these jobs, say, as a teacher or nurse. One of my other sons, Bryce, is a teacher, working with younger students. As a man, sometimes he has had to work extra hard to pursue this dream. He has not always been encouraged by others. But he is not going to let other people's views stop him. Nor will you, I hope.

Men can be nurses. Men can be teachers. Jermar Rountree from Washington, D.C., was a finalist for National Teacher of the Year and loves his job. He says, "I love what I do, and that will not change. I am dedicated to my kids, families, and colleagues. I want to be that trusted person, that father figure, that coach that my students can rely on no matter what."

Did you know that John Adams, the second president of the United States, was a classroom teacher? So was Archbishop Desmond Tutu, a hero to the people of South Africa for his fight for justice.

These are men who matter, whom you can count on. They offer a helping hand, not a clenched fist. They are brave men doing hard work to make life better for all of us. They are providers of care, love, practical assistance, safety, and learning.

Men can be psychologists or counselors, helping people who are sad or lonely. Men can be social workers, helping families and people who are in trouble. These are men like Warren McAdams, who went from being a volunteer firefighter to making it a career, often helping families with sick children, and men like Josh Bower, a police officer in the K9 unit working with dogs who became a counselor so that he could help people before they got into trouble, rather than afterward.

Lots of the men who choose these jobs, which some people insultingly think are "women's jobs," are proud of their work. Nurse Ben Medina says, "Nursing as a career has been such a blessing. It is a fantastic, amazing profession. Every day I'm excited to go to work."

Teachers, counselors, nurses. These men are heroes, I think, in a different but equal way to firefighters and pilots and soldiers. They know they are making a difference in other people's lives. They are pillars of strength in the lives of people who need them most. Maybe you could be one, too. Why not?

—Richard V. Reeves

Walt Whitman

Literacy: Poet

Sometimes, when someone is recognized for one aspect of their life, this one role overshadows their other important accomplishments. For example, Walt Whitman, one of the most important American poets of all time, was also a nurse. His experiences with patients influenced his poetry.

Unhappy Childhood

Walt was born on May 31, 1819, on Long Island, New York. He once remarked that he didn't have a happy childhood, with a family often stressed about how they would survive financially. To help with the family's income, he left school to find work at the age of eleven. Walt had several jobs, including as a teacher and a journalist.

Poetry for Everyone

In 1855 he published his first book of poems and started to become well-known for his poetry. He wrote poems about nature, friendship, and love. His goal was to write poetry for everyday Americans. Walt's book of poetry was revised, edited, and released several times during his lifetime.

The Civil War

When the Civil War broke out, Walt's brother George joined the Union army. One day, Walt was reading a newspaper when he saw his brother's name on a list of wounded servicemen. He immediately went to find him. When Walt found his brother—who had only minor wounds to his face—he saw so many other sick and wounded men. He decided that he had to be a part of helping these men at their lowest moments.

Volunteer Nurse

During the Civil War, Walt got a full-time job in Washington, D.C., but spent all his spare time as a volunteer nurse in army hospitals. At the beginning of Walt's time as a volunteer nurse, he brought candy and fruit to the injured soldiers and sat with them to hear their stories. He wrote letters for the soldiers to their families. He eventually cared for their battle wounds. After hearing their stories, Walt wrote poetry about his patients and sometimes mentioned the care he provided. Walt, a fan of President Lincoln, also wrote some of his most famous poems reflecting on the president's death.

Popularity

Though his poetry grew in popularity during his lifetime, it wasn't until his death that Walt's works were recognized more broadly. Walt passed away on March 26, 1892. Today, he is considered one of the greatest American poets of all time.

Go Give It a Try!

Our life experiences can inspire the creation of poetry. Consider an event from your life that was joyful, or a difficult and challenging experience, and write a poem that focuses on the five senses. What did you see, smell, touch, hear, and taste during this moment? Remember, the poem doesn't need to rhyme but should be an expression of one of your experiences.

c
4
1
e'
3
5
a
a
D

Joseph Lee

Arts: Culinary Arts/Baker

Bread is not something we spend a lot of time thinking about, as it is ever present in packed lunches, alongside meals, or on its own slathered with butter. We have one baker, Joseph Lee, to thank for our ability to have delicious, cost-effective bread.

Born Enslaved

Joseph was born in 1848 in Charleston, South Carolina. His parents were both enslaved, and so was Joseph. He grew up in South Carolina, learning to bake as a child while working at a bakery. Joseph didn't ever have a formal education, but he did go to some underground schools whenever he was able to. During the Civil War, he became a blacksmith, using heat to form metal. Then, Joseph became a cook on a ship, making his way north while improving his cooking and baking skills.

Baking as a Career

In Massachusetts, Joseph took a job in a bakery while selling food out of the boardinghouse where he lived. His breads and the other foods he created were delicious, and people took notice. Joseph opened his own restaurant while he was still in his twenties and began developing the Woodland Park Hotel in Newton, Massachusetts. The hotel was a resort getaway that grew in popularity and brought in wealthy and famous visitors, including three presidents.

Better, Quicker Bread

A skilled baker, Joseph wanted to create better, more delicious, and more efficient bread for his hotel. He set to work, dreaming up an invention that would take the strain and pain off the bakers he was working with and still produce a great product. Joseph developed an automated bread-kneading machine that saved time and resulted in better-quality bread.

Too Much Bread

Then the unthinkable happened: There was too much bread! With the help of Joseph's new invention, there was more bread than the staff could serve and his guests could eat. Joseph got to work again, inventing the automatic bread-crumbing machine. The day-old bread that would have been wasted was instead crumbled up to be reused in new ways. Modern-day breadcrumbs are used for frying fish, stuffing turkeys, or topping salads as croutons.

Long Overdue

Joseph sold his inventions to other companies, which made the baking industry even more efficient and cost-effective while limiting human failures often associated with baking bread. But his impact on the world was largely forgotten after his death in 1908. Then, in 2019 Joseph was inducted into the National Inventors Hall of Fame, noting his role in the great legacy of baking.

ARTS

Go Give It a Try!

Research how to make a loaf of bread. With the help of an adult, gather the ingredients and tools and try creating the bread by hand. As you do, pay attention to the muscles you use to create one loaf.

Forrest Spaulding

Literacy: Librarian

Walking into a library is magical—shelves and shelves of books of limitless topics and genres. There are books for almost every age and every interest. But what if that wasn't true? In the 1930s librarian Forrest Spaulding experienced the beginnings of censorship (when words or ideas are kept from others) and wanted to ensure that everyone had access to literature. His Library Bill of Rights proclaimed that everyone should have access to books.

Library School

Forrest was born on May 4, 1892, in Nashua, New Hampshire. As a young man, he moved to New York City and worked as a newspaper reporter. He then attended the New York Public Library's library school in 1913. Forrest began working in libraries in New York and New Jersey until moving to Des Moines, Iowa, becoming the city's librarian.

First Time in Iowa

While serving as the city's librarian, Forrest saw the importance of getting books into the hands of those with limited access, including men in the military. He organized a library at Camp Dodge in Iowa for World War I recruits. He then set up military camp libraries in other states. Forrest provided the soldiers with books on a wide range of topics and wanted all the books to be returned well used. In 1920 Forrest moved to the country of Peru. He oversaw the country's libraries and museums while working as a reporter for the Associated Press.

Back to Iowa

While in Peru, Forrest worked to provide news from the country but was often met with censorship. In 1927 he returned to his role as the Des Moines Public Library director and brought with him new and creative ideas, such as recording library programs for the radio airwaves. As the Great Depression hit the country, Forrest did his best to make books available to everyone and established the "Waterfront University" in the library's basement. This wasn't a real university but a place where men without work could find resources to further their technical and job-related learning.

The Library Bill of Rights

Forrest became angered by the United States's first censorship of library books. Elsewhere in the world, books were being banned and burned in great numbers because of their content. In 1938 Forrest drafted the Library Bill of Rights, which focused on an unbiased (without opinion) book selection, a balanced collection, and open meeting rooms. The library board accepted Forrest's statements and proclaimed they would not be bullied into censorship. Soon after, the American Library Association adopted the Library Bill of Rights for the nation. Though the document has been edited and updated based on current advances, the basic principles continue to this day. Forrest died on December 9, 1965, living a life dedicated to books and the freedom of expression and learning.

Go Give It a Try!

Do you have a library card for your local library? Start by getting one; it is free and easy. Learn about all the benefits of your card beyond checking out physical books. Many libraries have events, guest speakers, technology and equipment rentals, study spaces, tutoring, and digital downloads of audiobooks—and yes, books, access to a world of books. Visit your local library today.

Arthur George Smith

Arts: Jewelry Artist

Where do artists find their inspiration for their masterful works of art? Inspiration can come from anywhere: nature, our experiences, the people in our lives, and the world around us. Artist Arthur George Smith's jewelry designs found their beginnings in sculpture and dance.

Early Recognition

Arthur, known as Art, was born in 1917 in Cuba to parents who had emigrated from Jamaica. At the age of three, the family moved to New York City. At a young age, he showed artistic talent. In the eighth grade, Art won an honorable mention in a poster contest sponsored by the American Society for the Prevention of Cruelty to Animals. He was encouraged to attend art school, and he did, receiving a scholarship.

Inspired

In art school, Art was one of a small number of Black students. His advisers tried to push him to pursue architecture, suggesting he could get a job more easily in that profession. However, the mathematical precision of this field wasn't interesting to Art. He instead focused on sculpture. Upon graduating from art school, Art began taking night classes in jewelry making. Art became friends with another Black jewelry designer, Winifred Mason, who became his mentor and hired Art as a full-time assistant. Now, Art could learn alongside someone successful in this field who even owned their own studio and store. Art was inspired.

On His Own

In 1946 Art decided to make his move and opened his own jewelry studio and shop on a street with primarily Italian neighbors. He suffered racial violence from his neighbors, who threatened him, made him feel unwanted, and smashed his store windows. Art moved his shop to a new, more inclusive neighborhood, and his business thrived. Not only was he selling his work in his store, but his artistic jewelry was sold in craft stores in multiple cities. In the 1950s major retailers such as Bloomingdale's made his work available to a broader public.

Dance

The jewelry that Art designed was big and sculptural. The world of dance and music inspired him. He was hired to design jewelry pieces for innovative Black dance companies. His work got even bigger and more theatrical, featuring silver hand hammered into creative forms. The dancers' bodies made his designs come to life. Significant fashion magazines, including *Vogue*, featured Art's designs. Art even had the remarkable opportunity to design a brooch for First Lady Eleanor Roosevelt and cuff links for the musician Duke Ellington.

Legacy

Art's health declined in the late 1970s, which brought on the closing of his shop in 1979. In 1982 he passed away. His legacy continues as his oversize sculptural jewelry pieces are a part of museum and gallery collections.

Go Give It a Try!

Gather scissors, glue or tape, string, cardboard, and items destined for the recycling bin. Consider how you will use these found materials to make large jewelry pieces like necklaces or bracelets. Who will wear these pieces: you or someone else? Get cutting, gluing, and attaching to create your own theatrical jewelry items.

Mikhail Baryshnikov

Arts: Dancer

It can be easy to accept that we do things as they have always been done, to stay the course and not make things too complicated. But what happens when we seek innovation (creativity) and excellence? Mikhail Baryshnikov is seen as one of the world's greatest ballet dancers, who continues to leap toward new possibilities for himself and the whole artistic community.

Early Studies

Mikhail was born on January 28, 1948, in the Soviet Union, in what is now known as the country of Latvia. His mother introduced him to the arts, including music, theater, and ballet. At the age of twelve, Mikhail began studying ballet. A few years later, he won the top prize at an international ballet competition.

Frustration and Escape

Mikhail joined the Kirov Ballet and was recognized for his incredible talent. But he was also frustrated. The ballet companies in the Soviet Union staged only performances that stuck to traditional forms of ballet and dismissed new and creative dances created by those from outside the country. Mikhail grew tired of the rules placed on him as an artist. In 1974, while touring with other dancers in Canada, Mikhail was able to escape. He declared he was never going back to the Soviet Union and was seeking asylum. Those who ask for asylum believe they are unsafe in their home country and are seeking the protection of another country. Mikhail was allowed to live in Canada and joined the ballet company there.

Dancing and Directing

Mikhail joined American ballet companies, learning from coaches and directors that only made him a stronger dancer. He had the most impressive leaping ability, allowing him to dance complicated choreography (the steps of a dance) with elegance and power. After some time, Mikhail joined the American Ballet Theatre as a dancer but also as an artistic director. An artistic director works to bring ballet performances to life, determining the vision and direction the dance company will go.

Innovation

Innovation drove Mikhail and his work. As a result, he cofounded a program called the White Oak Dance Project. This new modern dance company employed experienced dancers as part of a touring company, with Mikhail as director. Years later, Mikhail founded the Baryshnikov Arts Center in New York City. This creative space supports different types of artists to explore, create, and perform their works with artistic freedom.

Stage and Screen

Known as one of the greatest dancers of all time, Mikhail received many awards, including the National Medal of the Arts. Beyond his direction and advocacy for artistic expression, Mikhail has acted on the stage and in TV shows and movies.

Go Give It a Try!

Mikhail was an exceptional leaper. Gather friends or family for a competition to see how far you can each leap. Mark off where each person lands. Remember, the goal is to jump over a long distance and not just up.

Gregor Lersch

Arts: Floral Designer

Flowers are tied to our emotions and the big moments of our lives. The right arrangement of thoughtfully selected flowers in a particular color can bring someone to tears and remind them there is beauty in the world. Gregor Lersch knows and lives this truth. And, he is well known for being one of the greatest floral designers in the world.

Generations of Horticulturalists

Gregor was born in 1949 in Bad Neuenahr, Germany. For more than 140 years and five generations, Gregor's family has been dedicated to floral design and horticulture (the art of gardening). His grandfather was one of the founders of a major flower delivery company. Gregor grew up surrounded by flowers and eventually studied at the Bonn Master's School in Germany. He became a florist (someone who specializes in designing and arranging flowers) himself.

ARTS

Award-Winning

In 1974 Gregor officially began his career with flowers. He entered his floral designs into various competitions, and in 1978 he won the European Cup, the first time a German had won this international flower competition. From then on, he actively participated in events and won countless awards for his creativity. Gregor didn't have a specific style that he continually relied on. Instead, he focused on creatively challenging himself with natural materials.

Sustainable and Organic

Gregor's interest is in the most natural forms possible: There should not be decorative items or fake flowers that take away from the real beauty of the flowers themselves and lead to further waste. But this does not mean that his works are plain or boring. His designs sometimes include branches, leaves, rocks, moss, and the most sustainable and organic flowers that he can get his hands on. Gregor's arrangements defy gravity, are inspired by cultures around the world, and constantly push the envelope of what is possible. He believes that all the elements of the design should eventually make their way back into the earth.

Teaching

While attending competitions and floral shows, and meeting other flower enthusiasts and beginning floral designers, Gregor knew he needed to share his knowledge and inspiration with others. He started teaching floral design classes in Germany and then expanded further until he began teaching courses around the world. He now speaks more than six languages to help him connect with others. His goal as a teacher is to help people see that designing with flowers should be as natural as the flowers themselves, that anyone can—and should—do it.

Recognition

Beyond his gold medals and championship wins at floral shows, Gregor was awarded the Order of Merit of the Federal Republic of Germany. This recognition is Germany's highest tribute to individuals who uplift society with their achievements in any field. For Gregor, the real reward has been the countless students who have enthusiastically listened to his guidance and have gone out to make the world even more beautiful.

Go Give It a Try!

Gather some flowers (you can purchase these at a grocery store if you can't find any outdoor flowers you are allowed to cut), some branches, leaves, and other natural items. Experiment with creating an arrangement by combining different elements in a vase or jar. Use scissors to adjust the height of the flowers and branches as you try out new possibilities.

Sir Ken Robinson

Literacy: Teacher
Arts: Advocate

What if kids are born curious and creative, but as they grow up, they aren't encouraged to practice these skills in school and lose the joy of creativity? That is what Sir Ken Robinson, an educator and advocate for arts education, witnessed. And his work has inspired countless educators, schools, and students worldwide.

Life-Threatening Beginnings

Sir Ken was born on March 4, 1950, in Liverpool, England. At the age of four, Sir Ken got polio, a life-threatening virus that can cause someone to not be able to move parts of their body, or even to die. He spent eight months in the hospital battling polio. His dad was a semi-pro soccer player and had thought that his son would follow in his footsteps. But polio had affected Sir Ken's strength and stamina, leaving him in a wheelchair for some time. So, upon returning home, his parents encouraged him to focus on his education.

Education

At first, Sir Ken's parents sent him to a school for students with disabilities. With his determination and his parents' encouragement, he excelled, moving from school to school. When he was sixteen, Sir Ken and some friends wanted to perform a play and worked after school for weeks with a teacher as a director. At one point, the director stepped away from the project and named Sir Ken, a teenager, as the new director. He was shocked but took on the responsibility joyfully. He then decided to get a degree in education, focusing on the arts, especially theater.

Teaching and Researching

Sir Ken began his career in education as the director of the Arts in Schools project, striving to develop arts education all over England and Wales. He worked as a professor of education, researching the importance of creativity in a student's education and for their success in the future.

Global Influence

Sir Ken believed teachers should support their students' individuality by promoting curiosity. He knew that students could discover talents they didn't think they had by trying new things. Sir Ken wanted all schools to focus on awakening the creativity that students are born with. So, he wrote books and gave presentations. He gave three TED Talks, inspiring videos about technology, education, business, science, and creativity. His talks have challenged educators and schools to prioritize creativity and curiosity. At one point, one of his videos was the most-watched TED Talk of all time. In 2003 Sir Ken was knighted by the Queen in recognition of his dedication to the arts. Sir Ken passed away on August 21, 2020. His influence on education was global and continues to impact teachers and students to this day and long into the future.

LITERACY

ARTS

Go Give It a Try!

Do a creativity workout with a partner. Have your partner draw a crazy shape on a piece of paper. Now it's your turn to take that shape and transform it into a new drawing. Now draw a shape for your partner and have them do the drawing. Work back and forth together, challenging each other's creativity.

Ralph Fletcher

Literacy: Author and Writing Advocate

We can get self-conscious about our ideas to the point that we don't share them with others because we fear they aren't good enough or we will be laughed at. Author and writing advocate Ralph Fletcher thinks that to get better at writing, we have to have a place to process, plan, and write out all of our ideas, even if those words are just for us.

Family of Storytellers

Ralph was born on March 17, 1953, in Marshfield, Massachusetts, the oldest of nine kids. He had a big family with many aunts and uncles who would gather and tell rich, beautiful stories. Though Ralph loved listening to his family's tales, his favorite stories involved sports. Ralph wanted to grow up one day to be the center fielder for the Boston Red Sox.

A Magical Job

As Ralph grew up, he loved reading. He thought about the writers of his favorite books and how incredible it was that they sat down and wrote these stories for kids to read. But Ralph never even once considered becoming a writer himself. This job seemed magical and impossible for a kid like him. He had his dreams of baseball to focus on.

Poem for Processing

In high school, Ralph met teachers who encouraged him to do his own writing. And when he met teachers who weren't so encouraging, Ralph wrote in a notebook that he kept all to himself. When he was twenty-one years old, Ralph's brother Bob passed away in a car accident. Ralph had so many emotions, and he didn't know how to process them. He started writing poetry as a way to express all that he was feeling. The loss of his brother became the push and inspiration for Ralph's first novel.

Writer's Notebooks

Ralph loved writing so much that he wanted to share his love with others. He started by working with teachers in New York City, joining them in their classrooms and talking about new ways to excite their students about their own writing. One resource that he was really interested in was the idea of a "writer's notebook." What if there was a place for writers of any age to try out their ideas, make mistakes, and take risks before sharing that writing with other people?

Get Writing

Initially Ralph wrote a book about using a writer's notebook for adults. But the ideas he developed worked well with students, too! Soon, Ralph was sharing his idea for using writer's notebooks with teachers and schools all over the country. He wanted to inspire teachers and their students to see themselves as writers and to encourage students not to seek perfection but to enjoy the act of writing itself. Ralph became a champion of literacy (the ability to read and write) by encouraging other writers and future writers. The boy who never thought he could see himself as a professional writer has written more than twenty books for kids and young adults.

LITERACY

Go Give It a Try!

Begin using your own writer's notebook. You can start by writing poems, short stories about your life, made-up stories, jokes, or any type of writing. Collect your ideas and start thinking about which ones you want to develop further or feel brave enough to share with others.

LeVar Burton

Literacy: Advocate

The *summer slide* is a term that refers to how kids may lose some of the academic progress they made during the school year because they are not reading during the summer. One of the most excellent solutions to this challenge came from a TV show hosted by actor LeVar Burton. This show catapulted him into classrooms and living rooms around the country and into the role of a literacy (the ability to read and write) advocate.

Potential Futures

LeVar was born on February 16, 1957, in Landstuhl, Germany. He was born on an army base, as his dad was an army photographer and the family was stationed there at the time. LeVar grew up in California, where, at thirteen, he joined a seminary intending to become a priest one day. As a teenager, he realized this wasn't the future he wanted and turned to acting.

Acting Achievements

At the age of nineteen, LeVar broke into the world of acting. He starred in the television miniseries *Roots*. The award-winning miniseries told the story of one African man and his family over generations, during and after slavery in the United States. After that, LeVar had minor acting roles until he was cast as a character on *Star Trek: The Next Generation*. The show was a huge success.

Reading Rainbow

In 1983 LeVar started hosting and producing a show called *Reading Rainbow*. Each episode of the program featured excellent hand-picked picture books that were read out loud for viewers. Other activities and virtual field trips accompanied the book readings, and the show always contained recommendations for kids, narrated by kids. Sometimes, special famous guest readers joined LeVar's hosting. The series went on to win numerous awards, including twelve Emmy awards for LeVar himself.

A Legacy

LeVar promoted reading for an entire generation of kids and made it exciting. *Reading Rainbow* was on TV for more than twenty years. The memorable theme song of the show sparks memories of book read-alouds and LeVar's calming and enthusiastic voice. He has continued to work as an advocate for children's literacy and, in 2017, began a podcast called *LeVar Burton Reads*. With each episode, he reads a short story for adults, some of the very same adults who tuned in to watch him introduce exciting books all those years ago.

LITERACY

Go Give It a Try!

What book have you read recently that you think others would enjoy? Create a recommendation video to be shared with family and friends. Share the book's plot, say who would enjoy it, and reveal some exciting moments you enjoyed. Be careful not to give up the ending or any significant surprises. Share your video with others and ask them to do the same.

Peter H. Reynolds

Literacy: Author
Arts: Illustrator

When you throw a small pebble into a body of water, a small ripple begins. The ripple expands and expands further from that small beginning point. Peter H. Reynolds may not have thrown a pebble, but his "dot" has engaged people worldwide to consider their own bravery and limitless potential.

Early Publishing Career

Peter was born on March 16, 1961, in Toronto, Canada, along with his identical twin brother, Paul. At the age of three, the family moved to Massachusetts. Here the Reynolds brothers began their publishing career at the age of seven. Peter and his brother used their dad's copy machine to create comic books and newspapers. Peter was constantly doodling and developed his own unique sense of humor.

The Accidental Dot

Peter grew up to be an author and illustrator. Whenever he would introduce himself as an artist, he would hear, "Oh, I can't draw." These responses frustrated Peter because it just meant they hadn't really tried yet. One night in 2001, Peter sat down with his journal and immediately fell asleep. When he woke up an hour later, he realized his permanent marker had bled on the paper and made a large dot. This dot felt special. He signed his name and hung the dot above the fireplace.

The Storied Dot

From Peter's accidental dot, he started writing the book that would one day be called *The Dot*. In this story, a child who questions her drawing abilities meets a teacher who challenges her to be brave and see where a single dot could take her. Peter's book has been translated into numerous languages and inspired a series of books focusing on creativity, bravery, and self-expression.

International Dot Day

In 2009 Terry Shay, a teacher in Iowa, introduced his class to *The Dot* during a one-day celebration of creativity, courage, and collaboration. Their celebration took place on the book's publication anniversary, September 15. Since that day, each September more and more students and their teachers join in on International Dot Day. The day is a celebration around the world, with librarians, teachers, and students from more than 189 countries participating.

His Mission

The ripples continue from that pebble, that initial dot. Peter has gone on to write and illustrate numerous books. He has opened his own bookstore and works alongside his siblings to encourage creativity and learning for everyone. With all of his projects, Peter's mission shines through. He wants to tell stories that matter and dares us to reach for our full potential.

LITERACY

ARTS

Go Give It a Try!

Pointillism is a technique of filling the page with different colored dots that create an image based on how close they are together or overlap. The most famous pointillism image is *A Sunday on La Grande Jatte*. Use markers to create a pointillism picture made entirely of dots.

Mo Willems

Literacy: Author
Arts: Illustrator

Cartoon animals with speech bubbles have taught countless kids that we all experience a wide range of emotions and that being silly doesn't have to stop when you "grow up." Author and illustrator Mo Willems has had a career that includes television, theater, books, and art exhibits. His illustrated world reminds us of the power of reading, writing, and drawing.

The Peanuts

Mo was born on February 11, 1968, in Des Plaines, Illinois. When he was four, his family moved to New Orleans. Mo loved drawing, and his favorite thing to draw was the characters from Charles Schulz's *Peanuts* cartoons, Charlie Brown and Snoopy. He would dream up his own stories for these characters and create his own cartoons. A five-year-old Mo wrote Charles Schulz a letter containing the line, "Can I have your job when you're dead?"

The Street

Won't you tell me how to get to Sesame Street? Mo knows how; he started working for *Sesame Street* as a writer and animator for nine seasons, earning him six Emmy awards. He later created two animated series and worked as a head writer on another. Mo decided to take a break from television to focus on his writing career.

The Pigeon

In 2003 Mo published his first book, *Don't Let the Pigeon Drive the Bus!* The book became a bestseller, was inducted into the Picture Book Hall of Fame, and won a Caldecott Honor (an award for book illustration). Beyond a pigeon, Mo went on to write books about an elephant and pig duo, a misplaced rabbit, a baguette-obsessed frog, and so many more expressive characters. Mo allows his characters to experience and express a wide range of emotions that make them relatable to kids and adults alike. Remembering the childhood joy he experienced drawing Schulz's cartoons, Mo purposefully designed characters that kids could easily re-create with simple shapes. He wants his readers to dream up new possibilities for his characters and their own silly stories.

The Kennedy Center

The Kennedy Center is the National Cultural Center for the United States, located in Washington, D.C. In 2019 the Center named Mo their first-ever education artist-in-residence. In this role, he developed programming and wrote musical theater productions based on his books. When the COVID-19 pandemic hit the United States in 2020, Mo produced a video series called Lunch Doodles with Mo Willems! He aimed to entertain and engage his audience with drawing, humor, and a glimpse into his world as an author and illustrator.

LITERACY

ARTS

Go Give It a Try!

Take a look at Mo Willems's characters. Use simple shapes to draw one or many of them in a completely new situation. Create a comic strip, a short book, or an artistic masterpiece. Go ahead, Mo would want you to!

Kwame Alexander

Literacy: Poet and Author

Everyone has different experiences with books during their childhood. Some kids have a few special books they reread over and over again. Others are surrounded by countless piles of books collected over time. And still, some kids don't own a single book. Poet, author, and literacy (the ability to read and write) advocate Kwame Alexander believes in the power of the written word to change the world, working to bring powerful books into all kids' lives.

Surrounded by Books

Kwame was born on August 21, 1968, in New York City and grew up in Virginia. During his childhood, he was surrounded by books because his dad was a writer and publisher and his mom was an English teacher. Reading was an important part of his childhood experience, but Kwame didn't want to read anymore. He wanted to play basketball. It wasn't that he hated reading; he hated being forced to read specific books instead of choosing his own reading material. Young Kwame created his first poem at the age of twelve. When he went to college, he considered a future in medicine. His plans changed when he took a writing class with the famous poet Nikki Giovanni. He was hooked.

Books and Book Festivals

The books that Kwame writes are for all sorts of audiences, including children, young adults, and adults. He writes stories, novels, and poems. Many of Kwame's characters reflect the lived experiences of African Americans, and his poems are responses to his own life and relationships. Frustrated by how national book festivals had few authors of color, Kwame decided to take matters into his own hands. He developed a book festival to reach diverse audiences and feature African American authors. The festival, named Capital Book Fest, started small and then expanded to several cities in the United States and the Caribbean.

Advocacy Work

Poetry can change the world. This is what Kwame believes. He works as an advocate for literacy around the world. Kwame started two organizations, one promoting creative writing and publishing for students. He has helped guide thousands of student authors in the United States, Canada, and the Caribbean to see their potential as writers. Another of Kwame's initiatives focuses on providing literacy support for students and their teachers in Ghana, Africa. He brought twenty other writers and activists to Ghana, where they delivered books, built a library, and offered professional learning opportunities for more than three hundred reading teachers. The team secured scholarship money to provide girls with the opportunity to attend high school.

Many Projects

Beginning with his success as a writer, Kwame's interests and involvement continue to expand. He won several significant awards, including the Newbery Medal, for his best-selling works. Kwame partners with schools and communities as a guest author. He is now producing television programming for kids and adults as well as podcasts, all with a passion for inspiring engagement with the written word.

Go Give It a Try!

As the poet-in-residence for the radio show *Morning Edition*, Kwame would provide the audience prompts to respond to, which he would then combine into poetry. Have your family members respond to one of Kwame's prompts, "Love is . . ." Collect all their responses and connect the lines to form a family poem. Don't forget to contact distant relatives via a call or text.

Dean Vendramin

Literacy: Teacher

Math can be fun. Math can provide you with opportunities to practice your creativity, problem-solving, and teamwork. This is what teacher Dean Vendramin believes, and he uses creative approaches like video games to make it all happen.

Rooted in Regina

Dean was born on June 10, 1971, in Regina, Canada, where he attended elementary, high school, and even college. As a kid, his parents modeled the importance of helping others and how good it feels when you made a positive difference. Dean realized it was true; helping people brought a sparkle to his eye. And who helps others? Teachers.

Math Teacher

Dean became a high school math and social studies teacher in the same city of the school that had taught him so much as a kid. But he kept thinking he couldn't teach his students the same way he had been taught. Dean knew that in the future, his students would be faced with challenges and opportunities that don't even exist yet. He began to think of new ways to teach and engage his students.

Minecraft

At home, his two sons were playing one of their favorite games, Minecraft. In the game, whole worlds were being built brick by brick, but there was also the potential for so much math learning. Dean created a new way to teach math that focused on real-world challenges while using a virtual format. He gave students assignments to design roller coasters and water parks and re-create famous architecture around the world. Students started using pencil and paper to plan their designs and then transferred their work to the game. While they placed blocks, they were learning math concepts such as slopes, grades, and trusses while flexing their creativity and problem-solving skills. And sometimes, taking the work one step further, they would bring their creations to life using a 3D printer.

Coaching

As a kid, Dean played with several sports teams and knew the power of learning to work as a team. Now a teacher, he decided to coach several different sports for his community, offering students opportunities to enhance their confidence and collaborative efforts: football, baseball, badminton, and weight lifting, as well as several clubs. But his newfound classroom efforts had Dean investigating a new coaching opportunity in eSports. His team would practice multiplayer games that brought them to local and national competitions. The students were learning about leadership, sportsmanship, and digital citizenship.

Recognition

Dean has been recognized as an exceptional teacher for his work with students, receiving awards and fellowship roles. He was named to the Minecraft Global Mentor Program. In 2023 Dean was honored as the recipient of the Prime Minister's Award for Excellence in Science, Technology, Engineering, and Math.

LITERACY

Go Give It a Try!

Design a roller coaster. Begin by planning your roller coaster on paper. Is this a wild thrill ride or a calmer traditional roller coaster for families? Then, build your roller coaster using a digital program, paper, or found objects around the home.

Carlos Acosta

Arts: Dancer

The word *ballet* often prompts images of pink tutus, satin shoes, and ribbons. But what about a strong Cuban man who started with very little and then went on to dance across stages worldwide? Carlos Acosta takes the stage.

Incredibly Energetic

Carlos was born on June 2, 1973, in Havana, Cuba. The youngest of eleven kids, Carlos's family had so little money that he grew up without toys and didn't have a birthday cake until he turned twenty-three years old. His dad noticed that his youngest child was incredibly energetic and worried that his energy would get him into trouble, so he enrolled him at the National Ballet School of Cuba. Carlos's dad hoped the school would teach him discipline, but never would he imagine where this decision would take his son.

Gold Medal Status

Carlos excelled in his dance studies. In 1990 he won the Gold Medal at the Prix de Lausanne, an international ballet competition for young dancers fifteen to eighteen years old. For those who participate in this unique competition, there are exciting possibilities. And, for students like Carlos, who won a Gold Medal, the world is open to them. At eighteen, he became the youngest-ever principal dancer with the English National Ballet in London.

Choreography

The Houston Ballet was his home for several years, where he further developed as a dancer. But it was with London's Royal Ballet that Carlos continued to flourish as a dancer and choreographed his own ballet for the company. When someone choreographs a dance, they design the movements the dancers make. Carlos even proudly brought the ballet company to his hometown of Havana for the very first time.

Tocororo

Carlos continued dancing for years as an international guest artist, joining ballet companies around the world. In 2003 he premiered a ballet he choreographed based on his life called *Tocororo*. The ballet opened in Havana and later broke box office records when it was performed in London. Carlos established his own dance company in Havana called Acosta Danza. He tours the world with his dancers, directing and performing alongside them. Carlos hopes that with his dance company, he can further share the vibrant culture of Cuba with the world.

Go Give It a Try!

There are countless proven benefits for those who learn ballet, including flexibility, strength, and balance. Search for ballet stretching routines online and begin to feel the benefits of this dance form. Are you enjoying yourself? Investigate local ballet classes.

Stephen Wiltshire

Arts: Visual Artist

Sometimes, all we need is a champion to notice us and celebrate our abilities beyond our current circumstances. Stephen Wiltshire began his life without communication until he picked up a pencil and began drawing.

Paper and Pencil

Stephen was born on April 24, 1974, in London to his two parents who were originally from the West Indies. At the age of three, Stephen was diagnosed as autistic. He didn't speak or communicate with his family or others in his life. After he enrolled in school, the teachers noticed that the only activity Stephen was interested in was drawing. He would draw animals, buses, and buildings, all with incredible detail. To prompt Stephen to speak, his teachers would make him ask for access to art supplies. His first words were *paper* and *pencil*. It wasn't until the age of nine that Stephen could fully speak.

Taking Notice

The school was buzzing with enthusiasm about Stephen's work, especially the sketches he created of significant London buildings. One of Stephen's teachers became his champion, accompanying him to art exhibits, entering his work in competitions, and going on field trips so that he could draw. Now, other people started to notice his beautifully detailed work, and the media (including newspapers and television) started featuring his art. His drawing of Salisbury Cathedral, a famous cathedral in England, brought him even more attention.

Skyline Sketches

Stephen was able to create highly detailed drawings of famous buildings and skylines. Soon, Stephen was invited to draw cities across the globe, impressing everyone with his ability. During a visit to Hong Kong, Stephen went up in a helicopter to view the city from above. The ride was only twenty minutes long, but when he touched back down to the ground, he started on a drawing that would become more than thirty-two feet (10 m) long. He could recall the tiniest detail and include it in his massive drawing.

Global Personality

Stephen's photographic memory (the ability to remember things exactly as they are seen or read) and the ability to draw what he had seen sent him to Australia, Mexico, China, Rome, New York, and more. But cityscapes aren't the only subject that Stephen draws. He creates more drawings of people within a year than buildings. He fills his private sketchbooks with caricatures of his close friends and celebrities. In 2006 Stephen was named by Queen Elizabeth II as a Member of the Order of the British Empire for his remarkable dedication and service to the art world. Later that year, he opened his own art gallery and studio, welcoming visitors by appointment. This artist, who couldn't fully communicate through spoken word until he was nine, was now an art phenomenon around the world.

Go Give It a Try!

Drawing from memory is an excellent way to boost your awareness skills, regardless of your drawing ability. Look at your living room for three minutes. Look for the details you don't always notice. Then go into the other room and draw everything you can remember. When you are done, head back to the living room to see how well you captured this space.

Corey Bulman

Literacy: Teacher

If you could have one superhero power, what would it be? Did you happen to consider curiosity? For Corey Bulman, he believes his superpower, curiousness, has driven him to keep learning and growing throughout his life. It led him to teaching, where he empowers his students to question, listen, and learn.

Early Struggles

Corey was born on August 4, 1975, in Wisconsin. He wasn't the best of students in elementary school, Corey struggled with traditional learning in reading and math. But he had teachers who believed in him and his potential. Though he may have been challenged in class, he had a skill all his own, one that may not have come naturally to his classmates. He was curious.

Trivia Time

As a kid, a trivia game for adults became super popular. Corey sat reading each card and memorizing the answers. He would later challenge adults to play the game. At first, Corey questioned if learning the answers from the cards was a form of cheating until he realized he was actually learning from the game. Corey was interested in learning everything and anything he could. And here was a way for him to do just that.

New Skills

Corey's high school art teacher and theater director provided Corey with opportunities to challenge his curiosity and develop new skills. At the University of Minnesota, Corey questioned whether to pursue being a lawyer or become a teacher. Then, he stopped and asked himself, "Which role would have the greater impact on others?" He knew the answer. Corey became a high school English teacher in Minnesota.

Role Model

In his classroom, Corey provides students with opportunities to study literature and poetry. But each day, he models curiosity for them, too. He gives students the chance to share about their lives with him and one another. Corey knows that all his students, especially the boys he works with, need to see a role model who is empathetic (understanding and sharing the feelings and experiences of others), curious, and gracious. Corey listens with empathy to his students' stories of losing a loved one, a feeling he personally knows too well, having lost his son to cancer. When students question what they will do next after graduation, he remembers being where they are, too. He doesn't need to have all the correct answers anymore. There are no trivia cards to memorize in these situations, but he now knows the power of stopping and intentionally listening.

Five Minutes

Corey steps aside at the end of each school year, saying that he has shared as much as he can with his students. It is now their turn to share. Each student prepares a five-minute presentation on any topic that matters to them. The students share presentations on balloon animals, dance, music, or life without a beloved family member. The other students listen with empathy and amazement. Corey's curiosity is now contagious. In 2017, a long way from his early elementary years, he was recognized as Minnesota's Teacher of the Year.

Go Give It a Try!

Create your own trivia game to share with your family and friends. Focus on topics you know well or that you want to better understand. Consider whether you will use multiple-choice questions or statements asking players to consider whether the information is true or false. Develop rules for your game and enough questions for everyone to join in the fun.

Luke Haynes

Arts: Quilter

Wrapping blankets and sheets over the backs of chairs and propped-up pillows, a young Luke Haynes created forts in his living room. These forts and the safety and warmth they created prompted him to explore a future as an architect, but ultimately he became a quilter.

Temporary

Luke was born on September 28, 1982. His parents divorced when he was young, and he spent his childhood moving from state to state. He lived in seven southern U.S. states. Luke was curious, built with plastic bricks whenever he could, and pulled together family blankets for making forts. The homes they lived in always seemed so temporary, which prompted Luke to consider what safe, stable homes could look like and to pursue a future as an architect.

Architecture School

Architecture school seemed like the right fit for Luke. Through his studies, he was investigating how a building could provide comfort and stability. But, he realized that maybe there was a better way to create works that addressed what he was looking for. In 2002 Luke made his first quilt, and there was no going back.

Warmth

Luke taught himself how to sew. His architectural learning supported his new adventures with fabrics, leading him to experiment and manipulate his material. This art form that so easily brings to mind images of grandmothers and warmth on chilly nights spoke to Luke. He understood that quilts were often lovingly created for survival and warmth. Just as he did with architecture, quilting seemed like a way that he could create safe spaces.

Thrift Stores

Luke now finds himself revisiting the thrift stores like those he spent time in as a kid. But this time, it wasn't to find clothing for himself but to find materials for his quilts. He selects used clothes and materials to reference his past and spark memories for others through his quilts. When designing his quilts, Luke follows traditional patterns with a twist. Other times, his artwork features stylized portraits, french fries, balloon animals, and even Croc shoes.

Affirmation Quilts

Luke works with his wife, Nicole, on anonymous (without a name) quilting projects. Luke creates a usable quilt that includes a hand-painted note of affirmation from Nicole. Then, the two leave the quilt somewhere to be discovered, kept, and used by anyone who needs it. Luke and Nicole don't do this project to get attention; their names aren't even attached to the quilt. They hope that their work is found by someone who could benefit from the quilt's warmth and safety.

Go Give It a Try!

Have you ever tried sewing? Locate a thread, needles, fabric, and a pair of scissors. After threading the needle and tying a knot at the end of the string opposite the needle, practice a running stitch through a piece of fabric. Push the needle through, leaving small lines of thread that continuously go under the fabric and then over the fabric. You should create what looks like a dotted line. Once you get the hang of it, research simple sewing projects.

Candido Crespo

Literacy: Teacher
Arts: Visual Artist

Changes to our daily routines and expectations can prove challenging. But what if these changes spark a sense of creativity that becomes contagious? That is what happened to Candido Crespo as he went from being an artist and teacher to being an artist, teacher, and dad who inspires other male role models to get creative.

Choices

Candido was born on August 26, 1984, in East Meadow, New York. Like so many kids, Candido was asked repeatedly what he wanted to do with his future. In middle school, he wrestled with the idea that he wanted to be either an art teacher or a veterinarian. Candido couldn't make up his mind and then realized he didn't have to decide just yet. During high school, Candido faced some challenges requiring teachers to come alongside and help him. These caring teachers confirmed that he wanted to be a teacher and to pay it forward by supporting his future students through their challenges.

Curiosity and Love

Right after college, Candido was hired into his dream job, teaching high school art classes to predominately Latinx and Black students. Since then, he has taught intermediate, middle school, and elementary students. Even with new classes and students of different ages, the one thing that didn't change was Candido's teaching style, which centers on curiosity and love. Though he was providing students with artistic experiences, his goal wasn't to develop a ton of working artists but to give students the confidence to try new things, explore possibilities, and face challenges with the knowledge that he was on their side.

Art Making and Podcasting

While teaching in the classroom, Candido shares his art with his students. He wants them to see his creative process and the skills he has developed, that the creation of a work of art is not something just in history books. He creates paintings, drawings, digital images, and whatever inspires his creativity. Candido hosted a podcast called the *Everyday Art Room*; the audience was other art teachers who were learning alongside him as he engaged with guest artists and educators each week.

CreativDAD

In 2018 Candido became a dad, and he was nervous that he would lose his time to be creative and make art, an important part of his identity and well-being. As soon as his son could hold art materials, the two, father and son, would sit together and spend time being creative. Candido realized that his new art-making partnership with his son could inspire fathers and male guardians to sit and be creative alongside the children in their lives. Candido offers workshops and presentations with simple directions, materials, and a whole lot of space for men and their kids to be creative. As soon as Candido's son was old enough to attend the workshops, he was introduced to the families in attendance as the coteacher.

Go Give It a Try!

Consider which male role model in your life you would like to sit down and be creative with, using one of Candido's drawing prompts. Together, draw what an epic battle between a monster and a robot would look like.

wootube
Subscribe
123
Save

Eddie Woo

Literacy: Teacher

Empathy can be defined as understanding and sharing the feelings and experiences of others. When we empathize with others, we can think of ways to help them in times of need. That happened with math teacher Eddie Woo, who made decisions from a place of empathy that would take his impact beyond the four walls of his classroom and out into the world.

Opportunities

Eddie was born in 1985 in New South Wales, Australia. Earlier, his parents had come to Australia from Malaysia, seeking better education opportunities for their children. However, as a child, Eddie was bullied by other students because of his Asian heritage. In school, Eddie worked hard and excelled in his studies, especially math. With his exceptional grades and intelligence, Eddie could have gone on to almost any career; he chose teaching and never looked back.

Teaching with Empathy

Eddie became a math teacher. Throughout his studies, Eddie identified that math was a challenge to sometimes understand. His journey to grasp difficult mathematical concepts allowed him to develop empathy for his students who may have found math difficult. This empathy led him to teach with enthusiasm and creativity. In 2012 one of Eddie's students was battling cancer and missing a lot of school. This hit Eddie hard—his own family had been deeply affected by cancer when he was in high school. Eddie began recording his math classes for the student, who could take their time watching the videos to grasp concepts they would have missed. The videos were engaging and helpful, and Eddie decided to post them on YouTube, hoping they would help other students with challenging math concepts.

WooTube

His videos became known as WooTube, and before long, he had more than one hundred thousand subscribers and millions of views of his virtual math lessons. Students found Eddie's videos easy to follow, and with the virtual format they could pause and replay the lessons over and over until they further understood the content. Eddie's presence on the screen prompted his involvement in several television programs in Australia, including hosting the program *Teenage Boss*. In this show, teenagers were given control of their family's finances for a month, making all decisions about how money was spent and saved while learning lessons about responsibility and planning.

Recognition

Eddie has been recognized for his work with several awards and recognitions. He won the Australia's Local Hero Award, he gave the Australia Day address (the first classroom teacher ever to do so) in New South Wales, and in 2018 he was named a top ten finalist for the Global Teacher Prize. Through all the recognition, Eddie continues to lead from the classroom with empathy and enthusiasm.

Go Give It a Try!

Eddie hosted a show about teenagers learning about finances. Have a family discussion about the grocery store and how much money your family tries to spend each week on food. Work with an adult to set a budget for food for a week. Visit the grocery store with an adult and decide what to buy and what not to buy to stick to your goal amount.

Curtis Oland

Arts: Fashion Designer

How often do you consider your clothing and where the design and the materials come from? And what about when you are done wearing them? Where do those pieces of clothing go next? These are the thoughtful considerations that fashion designer Curtis Oland puts into the design of his theatrical clothing pieces as he pulls inspiration from his indigenous (native) heritage.

Magic and Imagination

Curtis was born in 1989 and grew up in the Okanagan Valley of British Columbia, Canada. His mother's background is indigenous, of the Lil'wat Nation, and his dad's heritage is Scottish. The family chose to live relatively off-grid. There was no cable, no Nintendo, no white bread. But there was magic and imagination. The family loved Halloween, and young Curtis saw this as a time to create new characters and explore new identities.

ARTS

Intro to Fashion

Curtis went on to enroll in college, where he studied sculpture. In his second year at school, he was introduced to fashion. He became interested in the history of costume design and fibers. He learned about new designers who combined fashion, sculpture, and expression. Curtis knew that he needed to be part of this world. He enrolled in fashion design school.

Cultural Inspiration

In his designs, Curtis draws inspiration from his rich cultural heritage and the mountainous landscape of his home. He thoughtfully uses raw natural materials like wool, silk, linen, organic cotton, and deer and elk skins, the traditional materials of the Lil'wat people. Honoring the natural strength of the materials, Curtis often uses the raw edges of the animal skins that others would throw away and finds beauty in the frayed edges of fabrics that other designers would clean up. Curtis wants his designs to cause us to consider how what we wear connects us spiritually, to one another, and to the land. In 2016 Curtis won the Emerging Menswear Designer Award at Toronto Men's Fashion Week, further propelling his unique work into conversations about contemporary fashion.

Cultural Stereotypes

Working in London, Curtis became aware that others had stereotypes and preconceived ideas of what it meant to be an indigenous person. He worked alongside other indigenous artists who used film, music, movement, and visual art to create a multimedia project that spoke of how their different indigenous nations shared common values but were distinctly their own. Curtis's goal for the collaborative project was to spark the viewers' awareness and hopefully start meaningful conversations about our experience with our own cultures.

Go Give It a Try!

Coming up with a new look doesn't mean you have to buy all new clothing. Using the clothes you already have, design a new look for yourself. Combine pieces you have never tried together before. Mix textures, solid colors, and prints to create a unique look that is entirely your own.

Henry Liang

Arts: Flutist

What if you became so interested in a new skill and then realized you were the only person in the country who could perform that skill? Wouldn't this make you want to inspire and share your talents with everyone? This is true for Henry Liang, a performer of the flute, the piccolo, and an instrument you may have never heard of before: the shō.

Early Musical Start

Henry was born in Guangzhou, China. At the age of six, he started playing the dizi, a wind instrument made of bamboo. Two years later, he picked up the flute. He had the opportunity to play with a youth orchestra in China before moving to Australia, where his dedication and love of music further developed with the guidance of exceptional teachers.

The Navy Band

In 2013 Henry enlisted as a musician in the Royal Australian Navy Band. The Navy Band has a long history in Australia and performs during significant ceremonies, engages the public with national pride, records albums of patriotic and original music, and upholds national traditions. Henry went to naval training and also practiced his music. He plays the flute and the piccolo with the band and has performed for many international leaders. From 2014 to 2017, Henry served as the president of the Flute Society of New South Wales.

The Shō

Henry became the only Australian musician actively specializing in the shō, a traditional Japanese wind instrument. The shō is made up of seventeen skinny bamboo pipes bundled together, whose history dates to the seventh century when it was used in Japanese royal courts. The musician breathes in and out through the mouthpiece to make sound with this unique instrument. In 2015 Henry traveled to Japan and studied the instrument with a leader in shō performance.

The Silkworm

The Australian Broadcasting Corporation provided funds for new Australian music to be created. This included Henry and his shō. Henry composed and recorded an album he created named *Mori*, which references the silkworm and is the Japanese word for "forest," the source of the bamboo used to make the shō. The musical suite has four movements or sections. Each represents a stage in a silkworm's life cycle and symbolizes our daily challenges and triumphs. When Henry was a child in China, he even had silkworms as pets; the creatures have a special place in his heart.

Practice

Even professionals such as exceptional artists, musicians, and athletes have to practice. This is true of Henry, who knows there are no shortcuts to achieving your best. With his instruments, he practices scales and long tones. A long tone is when you hold one note as long as possible while keeping a steady and clear tone. Even when the work can get frustrating, Henry relies on his love for creating and enjoying music to get him through.

Go Give It a Try!

Henry shares that musicians should not only practice, practice, practice, but they should also listen to lots of music all the time. Go online and search for "Henry Liang musician shō" to experience this unique musical instrument. Does this experience prompt you to want to try a new instrument?

Rufai Zakari

Arts: Visual Artist

Have you ever taken the time to consider how much trash you create in a day and where that trash ends up? Artist Rufai Zakari acknowledges our complicated relationship with the garbage we create and wants us to rethink what happens to our waste.

Toy Creator

Rufai was born in 1990 in Bawku, Ghana. As a kid, Rufai and his friends would collect pieces of garbage they found in the city streets. The kids would turn the collected bottles, food wrappers, and plastic bags into toys and sculptures.

Returning to Childhood

Rufai studied art in school, where he learned about painting techniques and then created street art with the mentorship of a well-known street artist. While using spray paint to create his work, he came across piles of garbage. These discarded materials sparked memories of his childhood when he would collect trash to create something new. He began including these found items in his artwork, exploring pollution and our role in its impact on our communities.

Portraits of Strength

The artworks Rufai creates are almost always portraits of women from his community. Their strength and resilience inspire him. He lovingly reimagines these women out of reclaimed materials. Rufai's portraits are created by stitching together the found plastic items, just as someone would sew pieces of fabric together to create a quilt. He doesn't hide that his art is made from found items but uses the colors and patterns found on plastic bottles and bags to create bold portraits.

Discovering Materials

When he first started repurposing trash, he would find the materials himself, and then his family members would help with the collecting. Now, he employs women and children in his community to help locate items, paying them for their efforts. Bawku, Rufai's hometown, has been deeply impacted by decades of conflict that left the city in ruins and resulted in many lost lives. But Rufai has hope for his community. He founded a nonprofit that pays community members for their efforts to find, clean, and provide materials for his artworks.

Global Conversations

Rufai's works are now exhibited in museums and galleries around the world. With his carefully stitched visuals, he can share his local community, the strength of its people, and our relationship with single-use plastics with the world.

Go Give It a Try!

Gather materials from your recycling bin or those ready to be thrown in the trash. Consider which ones you can work with safely and begin by playing with stacking, flattening, and folding the materials. Use limited additional materials (tape, glue, scissors) to assemble your found objects into sculptures.

Takeru "TK" Nagayoshi

Literacy: Teacher

An advocate is someone who publicly and boldly shows their support and recommends potential solutions or changes. An advocate sees something wrong and feels the need to use their voice and speak up. Takeru "TK" Nagayoshi found his voice and will continue using it to improve education for all students.

Lots of Change

TK was born on July 8, 1991, in New Jersey. His parents came to the United States from Tokyo. When he was nine, TK and his family moved to Japan because of his mom's job with the United Nations. In Japan, TK was faced with learning the Japanese language and attending a very different school setting than he was used to in the United States.

A New Challenge

At the age of fourteen, TK and his family came back to the United States. But now, he faced new challenges: His English language skills were rusty, and he lacked confidence in school. Thank goodness for great teachers who saw his potential and encouraged him throughout his learning.

Access to Diverse Literature

TK first studied international relations and then got a master's degree in education. He started teaching reading, writing, and research classes in Massachusetts. As an English teacher, TK thought back to the books he read when he was in high school. He realized that almost all the books were written by white men or featured main characters who were white. Characters of color were often minor characters. In the books he read in high school, he never encountered an Asian character, someone like himself. This truth led TK to provide his students with access to literature that was as diverse as the students in his classroom. He wanted to introduce all his students to the rich diversity of the human experience and to explore difficult topics together.

Advocacy through Writing

Advocacy became the cornerstone of TK's work. He advocated for excellent education for all students, specifically students of color. He wrote countless op-ed articles on education issues. An op-ed is a piece of writing that features the opinions of a knowledgeable author and are based on their lived experience. TK's writing was featured locally in Massachusetts and nationally.

Involvement and Recognition

TK believed in using his voice to advocate for students and teachers, and he would do just that. He served on committees, panels, and task forces centered on diversity and equity in education. Other media formats, such as webinars, podcasts, and radio interviews, helped him reach different audiences. He was named the 2020 Massachusetts Teacher of the Year in recognition of his efforts in and out of the classroom. He continues to write articles, book chapters, and op-eds that advocate for teachers and students, focusing on diversity and inclusion.

LITERACY

Go Give It a Try!

Visit your local library and ask a librarian to help you find your favorite type of books (graphic novels, mystery, magical adventures, historical fiction, and so forth) that feature diverse main characters. You may find a new favorite character or even a new author to continue reading.

Tom Daley

Arts: Knitter

A gold medal Olympic athlete and accomplished knitter, Tom Daley has become a hero in the world of diving and also champions the powers of knitting. Armed with knitting needles, yarn, and a sense of purpose, Tom breaks outdated stereotypes of who can be an accomplished knitter.

Competitive Diving

Tom was born on May 21, 1994, in Plymouth, England. He started diving at the age of seven when a coach noticed his talents. He was then entered into national and international competitions. At fourteen, Tom was the youngest British competitor in the 2008 Summer Olympics. He competed in other Olympic games, winning gold and bronze medals. Tom had become a household name, and his stardom only increased with each appearance in and out of the pool.

Just Be Still

One of Tom's coaches approached him about his restlessness. Tom was told he was terrible at sitting still while resting and recovering. He needed to find a way just to be still. So, in March 2020 Tom decided to try out knitting. Knitting uses large needles and loops of yarn that interlace with other loops to create all kinds of clothing and soft accessories. During a trip to Canada, he watched YouTube videos. How hard could it be? But he couldn't get the hang of it. Australian and Russian divers offered advice and support, as well as one of the coaches on his British diving team. Only then did he start to grasp how to knit.

The Purple Scarf

The very first thing that Tom completed with his new knitting skills was a scarf for his mom. It was purple, her favorite color. It started terribly, but with focus, he gifted the scarf to his mom on Mother's Day. With time and practice, Tom became more confident, and his knitting skills strengthened. He could take on more challenging designs and forms, even coming up with his own designs. Knitting became his escape. When Tom got out his knitting needles, he became calm and focused.

Olympic Gold

Due to the COVID-19 pandemic, the 2020 Summer Olympics were held in 2021 in Tokyo. Because of the pandemic, no fans other than fellow athletes were welcome in the stands. On TV, the world saw Olympic diver Tom Daley in action—in the pool and with his knitting needles. While cheering on other athletes, Tom was spotted knitting away in the stands. He created a complicated cardigan sweater with Olympic rings and the British flag. In Tokyo, Tom won a gold medal for diving and knitted a small pouch for the medal. On one side was the U.K. flag, and on the other was the flag of Japan, the Olympic site for that year. He shared that he could carry his gold medal around without it getting scratched.

Go Give It a Try!

You don't need a complicated design or needles to start learning how to knit. Finger knitting requires yarn and your very own fingers. Watch tutorials online, and though it might be challenging at first, practice and perseverance can bring a sense of accomplishment and focus.

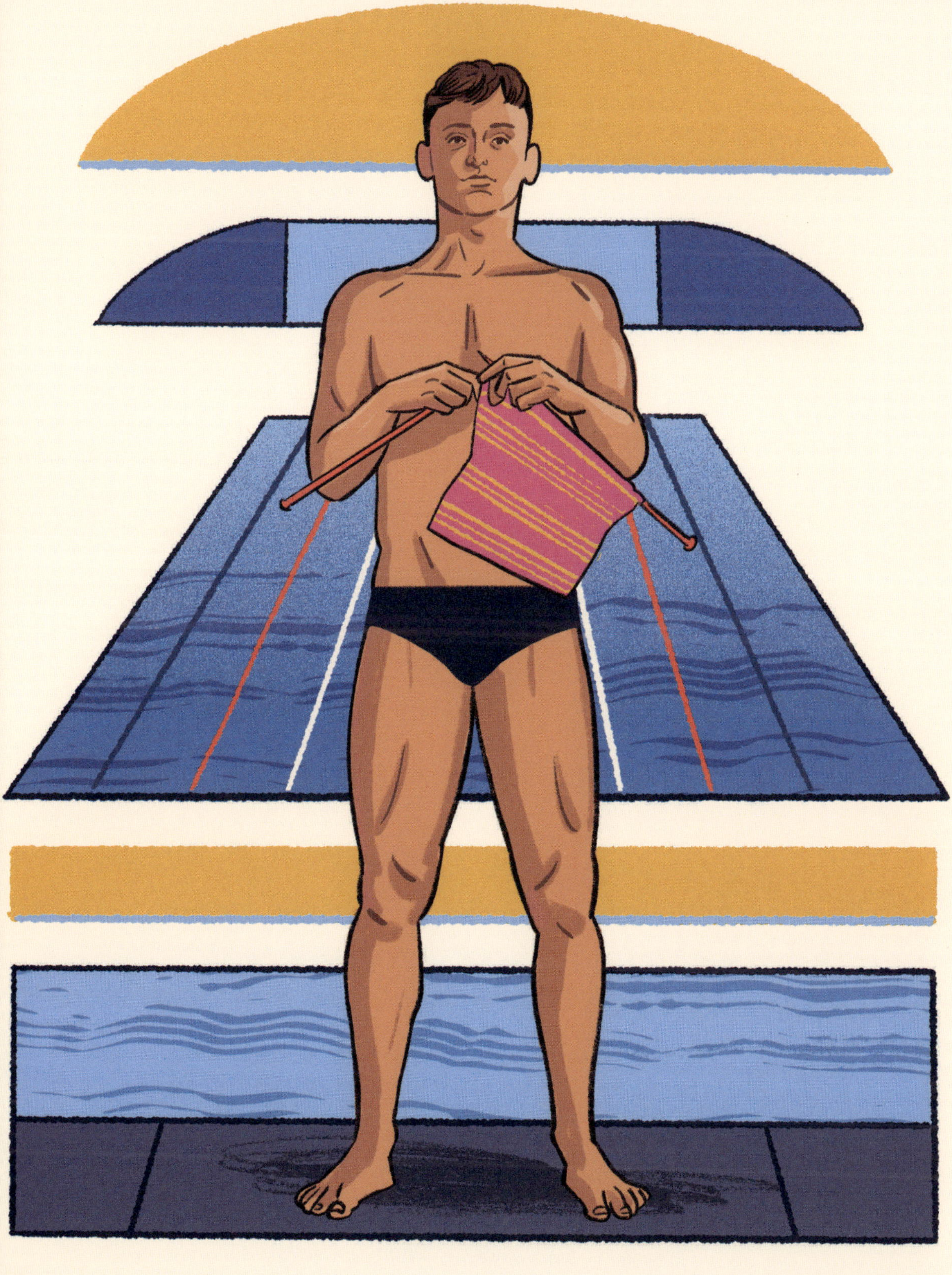

Kevin Aspaas

Arts: Weaver

Weaving is an art form that has roots in cultures and communities around the globe. The Navajo people, who prefer to be called the Diné ("The People"), have created weavings for centuries that connect them to the earth, their spirituality, and one another. Kevin Aspaas learned about weaving from his mother and honors his family legacy while making work that is all his own.

Weaving a Connection

Kevin was born in 1995 in New Mexico. When he was around eight years old, his mother began to teach him how to weave. She had learned from her sister, who had learned from their mother. Kevin started by learning how to weave simple sash belts. Weaving is a traditional art form in the Diné community, but not just an art form. Weaving provides warmth, clothing, and a connection to the earth and their ancestors. Kevin sat and heard stories about his grandmother as he learned to weave.

Weaving a Legacy

Weaving is an important part of Diné culture and history. Many generations ago, both men and women took part in weaving, but European settlers had more rigid gender systems and most recent weavers were women. When Kevin was a kid, he focused only on the weaving. He didn't know much about the rich culture and history associated with the art he was creating. Elders in his community taught him the importance of weaving beyond its beauty. Kevin decided to become a weaver to continue the legacy of his family of weavers, craftspeople, and storytellers.

Sheep-to-Loom

Kevin's grandmother owned a flock of sheep, which she cared for, and used their wool to create her weavings. In 2020, after learning weaving from his family, Kevin became dedicated to the traditional Navajo sheep-to-loom weaving process. He moved to Shiprock, New Mexico, on the Navajo Nation. Here, he has a flock of sheep that rely on him for their care. The seasons dictate the sheep's needs, and their care is reflected in the wool. Kevin knows that the weavings made from his sheep's wool will be stronger, more vibrant, and more powerful as he cares for them. But it isn't just the wool that he collects naturally. Kevin uses found natural materials to create his own dyes to make different colored wool for his weavings.

The Art

Navajo weavings grew in popularity after the railroad expanded through the Southwest in the late nineteenth century. However, only specific woven designs were deemed most marketable by traders. So, the Navajo weavers were limited in what they created and neglected traditional patterns. Kevin worked with another skilled weaver to learn these traditional designs and methods, incorporating them into his work. Beyond woven works of art that collectors and museums value, Kevin believes in the power of making works for others. He weaves traditional dresses, belts, and moccasins for members of his broader community.

Go Give It a Try!

Research how to make your own natural dyes with the plants and vegetables you have around the house. Search for tutorials online that explain which plants produce different colors. Test out your new dyes on white fabric and consider dying white T-shirts. Use a fixative to set the dyes so that they won't wash out.

About the Authors

Jonathan Juravich began teaching elementary art outside of Columbus, Ohio, in 2005. Still actively teaching art to young students, his personal and professional focus is on the importance of social and emotional learning in our daily lives. This is his favorite topic for research and discussion, including his PhD dissertation, his TED Talk "How Do We Teach Empathy," his limited-series podcast *The Art of SEL*, and his Emmy award–winning digital drawing program "Drawing with Mr. J." In 2018, Jonathan was named Ohio Teacher of the Year and one of four finalists for National Teacher of the Year. In 2023, he was named the National Elementary Art Teacher of the Year by the National Art Education Association. He lives in Columbus, Ohio, with his family.

Richard V. Reeves is the founding president of the American Institute for Boys and Men (AIBM) and the author of *Of Boys and Men: Why the Modern Male Is Struggling, Why It Matters, and What to Do about It*. Before founding AIBM in 2023, Richard was a senior fellow at the Brookings Institution. While at Brookings, he focused on policies related to economic inequality, racial justice, social mobility, and boys and men. He is also a regular contributor to the *New York Times*, the *Atlantic*, *National Affairs*, and other publications.

Between 2010 and 2012, Richard was director of strategy to the United Kingdom's Deputy Prime Minister. A former European Business Speaker of the Year, his other previous roles include director of Demos, the London-based political think tank, principal policy advisor to the Minister for Welfare Reform, research fellow at the Institute for Public Policy Research, and journalist for the *Guardian* and *Observer* newspapers. He earned a BA from Oxford University and a PhD from Warwick University. Richard tweets from @richardvreeves and his website is richardvreeves.com.

About the Illustrator

Chris King is an illustrator and artist from West Yorkshire, in the north of England, whose illustrations have an impactful style based on strong line work and a lifelong love for comic books. His figurative illustrations have led him to work for leading media outlets, publishing houses and consumer brands worldwide. When not drawing Chris can be found making music and walking the many moorland trails near his home.

Acknowledgments

This project would not have been possible without Richard Reeves' research and H.E.A.L. concept that challenges us to rethink stereotypes and possibilities. May this book serve as an inspirational resource to introduce our children to male role models in the fields of health, education, arts, and literacy who have made this world a more empathetic and beautiful place. To the men who are featured in this book, thank you for your work and for stepping into spaces with confidence, curiosity, and creativity. Thank you for sharing rich, vulnerable stories of your lived experiences. I am certain that your profiles will inspire future leaders and dreamers.

Thank you to Jonathan Simcosky and the Quarry Books team for their guidance throughout this process, and their dedication to this project. Endless gratitude to Chris King who breathed life into these profiles with his beautifully expressive portraits. And to my family, thank you for your unwavering support throughout all the seasons of our life together.

—Jonathan Juravich

Also Available

ISBN: 978-1-57715-674-1

ISBN: 978-1-57715-673-4

ISBN: 978-1-57715-672-7